PRESS4WARD

STEVE, THANK YOU FOR SHARING YOUR
STORY. CONTINUE TO PRESS4WARD IN
WHAT THE LORD HAS PRESS IN YOUR
HEART AND ALLOW HIM TO TAKE YOU
2 NXT LEVEL IN YOUR JOURNEY.

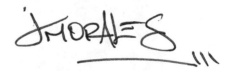

JOSE MORALES

NEWMAN SPRINGS PUBLISHING
320 Broad Street
Red Bank, NJ 07701

First originally published by Newman Springs Publishing 2020

ISBN 978-1-63692-156-3 (Paperback)
ISBN 978-1-63692-157-0 (Digital)

Printed in the United States of America

This book is dedicated to inspire you. Remember that adversity is never against you, but *for* you.

All my gratitude to everyone who supported and believed in me. For all the knowledge and wisdom that I received throughout making this book. With much love Compel America, thank you for the trust and support in allowing me to be part of something that I believe in and stand for.

To my best friend and my love of my life, Stephanie. Thank you for your unconditional love and putting up with me, I'm so blessed to have you in my life. I love you! To all my kids, the reason I continue to be a better loving father each day, and my lil' man Logan. You definitely made a difference in my life. Love you all!

To the organizations and people that helped
me make with this project possible:

-Newman Springs Publishing
www.newmansprings.com

-Compel America
www.compelamerica.org

-Lucindy Garcia, LG Photography
www.lucindygarciaphotography.com

-Mike Kogan
NEXUS Digital Marketing
www.nexusbeyond.com

-Yishmael Grossman

PREFACE

Let me begin here. I knew years ago that at some point down the road, I would be writing a book—but never in a million years would I have thought I'd be writing about my personal life story to inspire and motivate people. Had you asked me as a young child what I saw myself becoming when I got older, I would definitely not have seen myself doing anything I'm doing now being a motivational speaker.

As a child, I would have answered that I don't have a future and I don't know what I wanted to become. Don't get me wrong; I love to talk, but given the lifestyle I was living at that particular time, maybe I would say I wanted to be like my father which, in reality, was not a good thing at all—at least according to my mother. My mother was going through depression suffering daily and, on top of that, was dealing with my father who was a womanizer and drunk more than he was sober. He was high daily and also in and out of jail.

So when I was approached and encouraged to write this book by my mentor and friend, I really took it to heart and thought about it. I asked myself, what would I write and want people to know about me? I mean, I know I've been through a lot in my childhood and throughout my adult life. But who hasn't? I kept thinking over and over, *How can I make a difference in someone's life?* Even if it's for just one person, I would do it. I realized that there are a lot of broken families out there in this world that need to hear about hope and faith and that there are individuals who need encouragement. There are mothers, fathers, brothers, sisters, grandparents, uncles, aunts, cousins, friends, and workers who need to know that the adversity we all go through serves a purpose. Adversity and how we deal with it defines us. It's what makes us; it's what gives us strength to overcome future challenges.

No one goes through life unscathed. We all go through crisis; some more than others. Most of us have issues and challenges, and there is no one magic bullet or cure to all of them. Individual mentality and spiritually can help us handle what one is going through. So I thought about it and took my mentor's advice and started to write down what I did to overcome with adversity and how I continue to *press4ward and finish strong*.

1

- Compassion
- Acts of Kindness
- Empathy
- Respect

When I see these words or hear them, I would like to believe that these words define who I am today. I would like to believe that I am a compassionate person toward people who can't defend themselves. An act of kindness is something I have always done as long as I can remember—just doing something for someone because it is in my heart and expecting nothing in return. Just acting on it. I truly enjoy doing things for others, and that can make a significant difference in how they feel. Having the ability to understand and share somewhat the same experience or similar issues that other people are going through or have been through is a blessing to me.

Respect is another thing very important to me. Respect is letting people know that whatever our differences are, I show them that I respect them as a human being no matter what other people in their lives think of them. I get easily bothered with people who tend to treat others as if their lives' existence don't matter. For me, it's a horrible feeling you can instill in anyone. Respect is a two-way street. You treat others how you want to be treated. It shouldn't matter your nationality, culture, gender, or even those with special needs. We all should be treated equally. The sad truth is, we all know that is not the case everywhere we go. Nowadays, we encounter a lot of disrespect whether it is from our own family, friends, coworkers, shopping stores, or traffic lights. Oh, boy, let's not go there—even in the parking lot of a church. That's right. Even in the house of God, there is disrespect.

Many people don't realize the impact one can have on someone's life when you just acknowledge their presence. The crazy part is, it is free! It does not cost you any money, but certain people somehow act like it does. Do you know how powerful it is just to say "Hi?" It makes a world of a difference in their lives, not to mention your life as well. We don't know what people are going through in their home, work, family, relationship, or with their own identity. We can all relate to this. We all go through this at some point or another. Yes, some issues are very big; they are overwhelming, and there are small issues as well. In fact, some are so small you don't even know they are even there, but they are. Those also cannot be avoided because small things tend to grow and weigh us down.

When I talk about this, I can attest to this. I lived for too long as a child, teenager, and into early adult life being different.

I tried so hard to understand when I was a young child as to why I was treated in a certain ways—as if my existence was a bother, as if I did not belong, and as if I was a nuisance to my family and society. Sadly it was mostly from those whom I thought were my friends in my neighborhood or in school. What I am about to tell you, it's not about pity. I am definitely not looking for pity. I do not want you to miss the point of the message.

I remember one day I had something amazing happen to me. While I was busy complaining and blaming the world and every person that I can think of for my past and present failures, this still, small voice in my head was telling me "to shut up." I was confused at first, then I heard it again, and then bam! I felt like a ton of bricks had just fallen on me. I've been living my entire childhood up to my adult life blaming other people for my setbacks, my failures, and using my disability as an excuse for not getting what I wanted out of life. In other words, "I wasn't manning up to my responsibility." All I was doing was crying about the circumstances I found myself in. At no time did I even consider to stop and look at the one person who was really doing the most damage to my life. That person was me. I wasn't allowing myself to *press4ward* and accomplish anything in life. I was playing the victim card all these years, and all along, the one person that I needed to check a long time ago was myself.

Something about that day and that moment when I realized I had to ask myself, why in the world did I not figure this out sooner? What took so long? Did I not had the courage to face myself? Was I that blind? Why, when looking into the mirror all these years did I never take responsibility? I was only looking at my outward appearances and never seek deep inside within myself. When I had figured it all out, I felt relieved. I realized for the first time that I am worthy and I am much more than I give myself credit for. I was so occupied on this journey of self-pity that I did not realize that I always had a choice.

Once I started, the ball began rolling. I began with small steps. Day by day, I started to feel things getting very uncomfortable for me. I knew I had to choose and figure out what was allowed in my life that was positive and would better me. I also had to let go of the things and people that were a hindrance in my life. If I didn't, I would instead definitely fall back again, something I didn't wanted to repeat. I had to emotionally, mentality, and spiritually equip myself, but how was this was going to happen? By taking action for my responsibility. It had taken me this long too long to figure this out, and I wasn't going to start playing the same roll again. It had taken me so long to realize my plight and sorry life. I knew I needed to move forward from here on. Little by little, I was feeling less overwhelmed, but at the same time, I still hurt. I had to learn to let go of my past but not forget my past. These are two totally different things. You have to let go of what has taken place throughout your past, or else you can't move forward.

JOSE MORALES

Here's an example: say you were to have both of your hands occupied with two plates of food and you want to eat, but you can't because you don't have utensils. Then the opportunity arises and someone offers you utensils. You want them; in fact, you need them. In order for you to get the utensil, you must let go of one plate that you're holding on. It's the same thing in life. You need to pick and choose your *needs* or *wants* and how this will benefit you in the long run. Now my past shaped me into the person I am today. I had to learn to take my stumbling stones and turn them into my stepping stones and continue to *press4ward*. Take what's bringing you down, turn it around, and use it to your advantage. You're only living one life, but we are given many opportunities to do it right. It's never too late to start. Forget about the "What if I fail? What if you don't do something?" It's far worse to go through life wondering if you should have taken that opportunity when had the chance. By then it'll be far too late!

"You can't start the next chapter of your life if you keep reading the last one"—Camy Smith (BeUnlocked)

2

As a child, I was physically abused by my mother. Abuse was handed out on a basis. Some days weren't as bad as others. It all depended on what the problem was. Now my mother was never a drinker, so I couldn't blame a bottle. She never used drugs, so I couldn't blame a substance. So what was the cause? I'll get to that later.

I can remember when I was five or six years old when I was wondering why this was happening to me. What was it that I was doing to cause my mother to be so angry? At any given moment, I could get a smack across my head or the "Puerto Rican chanqleta." For those of you that do not know what that means, it's getting a whipping with the slipper. Then you had the "Puerto Rican pela." That, my friend, is the point of no return. She would use anything and everything that was within her reach. I say "within her reach" because she is only four feet and ten inches tall. But in those moments, to me, she was ten feet and four inches tall. It was insane how this little woman made the Incredible Hulk look minuscule. I am exaggerating, but it sure felt like it at the moment.

Then there was my father. A man who was in and out of my life for as long as I can remember. From my childhood to my late twenties when I found out that he had died, he exposed me to things you shouldn't expose any minor to, let alone a six-year-old. I was surrounded by alcohol, drugs, sex, and parties. Any time he would go out, he would always take me along with him. These were the only times that I was free from getting abused by my mother. My father, on the other hand, would tell my mother that if he ever caught her touching a hair on my head, he would put her six feet under, and he wasn't joking. I went everywhere with my father although the places he would take me were not appropriate. I didn't know any better because it was part of my life, so I didn't put much thought into it.

My way of escaping the life I had at home would be to draw almost all day long while watching nonverbal cartoons such as *Tom & Jerry*, *Mighty Mouse*, *Courageous Cat*, and *Minute Mouse*. I remember this sense of peace whenever I was doing any of these things, and then there was dancing. It was therapy for me, a way of coping with everything that was taking place at home. I was so damn hyper when I was a kid. I couldn't sit still, so I would dance until I was exhausted. The next thing I know, I'm awoken by my mother screaming at my father and my father yelling back. Then the sounds of my breaking furniture and my mother telling him to stop. That's when the beating came. My father would hit my mother, and I'd hear the door slam shut. He was gone. A few days would go by, and my mother wouldn't hit me. It was nice to be able to be around her while she was kissing me and hugging me. It felt so good to be loved.

Then my father would show up after a couple of days of not coming home for a few days. Everything would be like *Leave It to Beaver* family and then BAM! We would go through the cycle again which lasted for a couple of years.

3

There were many times when I was a younger child that I wondered why I was even alive. Am I worth anything? I was trying to reason why all this was happening in my life. Did something I do cause my parents to always fight? Was it my fault?

Then there were times there was so much love at home. I felt something inside of me; it felt so right. I would take advantage of those moments and enjoy being around my mother. Still to this day, I remember sitting on my mother's lap. I would rest my head on her chest, and I would feel at peace. Something about hearing her voice, hearing her heartbeat was soothing to me. Times like this, what made me feel alive was feeling like I belong. Despite of all the beating I got from her, somehow, these moment made up for it.

My mother was a housewife. She was very young when she had me at the age of seventeen. She gave birth to me on March 6, 1971, in Lincoln Hospital in the South Bronx of New York City. This is what I should feel like, and I would not want to let go of that fleeting moment. My father loving my mother and my mother loving my father. We would dance and joke around. It all was good up to the point that my father would want to go out and take me along.

As I started to get older, times like this would stress me out. I knew why he wanted to go out and what would happen once we got back home. I no longer looked forward to going out with my father. We would go to the city to hang out with his friends. We were not going to see a ball game or to play cards or dominoes. Nope, we would be in the garage where my father worked. He was an auto body mechanic, and hanging out would consist of me watching my father along with his friends drink beer and do white line. For those of you who don't know what white line is, it's cocaine. It could be ten o'clock in the morning or ten o'clock at night; it was always around. Then he would take me to various women's apartments. I was the kid who would entertain the woman's child by playing while my father would have sex with these women. This would go on throughout the day with him drinking and sniffing white line. We would head to another woman's place, rinse, and repeat.

The irony is, as I got older, in my late teens, I found out that all these children I was playing throughout my childhood were my brothers and sisters.

4

I should tell you about the South Bronx circa early 1970s. In six words, the South Bronx was a jungle. Things were bad and worse. The area was riddle with crime and poverty. Dozens and dozens, perhaps hundreds of buildings were abandoned and unemployment was extremely high. When combined, these elements produced a strong attraction for gangs. Gangs came in a variety of colors, but they had one thing in common: crime!

Gangs and their members supported themselves by selling drugs. With drugs and drug abuse came other crimes including armed robbery, assault, arson, rape, and of course, cold-blooded murder.

My family live by Simpson Street in an area of the Bronx then known as "Fort Apache, the Bronx." A regular day in the area featured most of the elements I just listed.

I recall vividly the blackout in the summer of 1977. I was seven years old. It was hot, sticky, and dark inside, so we hung out on the fire escape where in front of my eyes, I witnessed officers of the NYPD trying to beat up on my uncle

Carlos. Today everyone has cellphone that can record these events. Back then and young as I was, all I could do was yell for my mother. And I did. I yelled out that the cops were beating on Uncle Carlos with their nightsticks. Thankfully, they didn't shoot him. By the time my mother came out, Carlos managed to escape and run across the street and into our building.

Incidentally, our neighborhood was also the birth of hip-hop music. Hip-hop music arose in the 1970s when block parties became increasingly popular in New York City. Hip-hop is a broad conglomerate of artistic forms specific subculture within South Bronx, particularly among African American and Latin American minorities that were residing in the Bronx. DJ Kool Herc were the first to introduce this style of music and is considered the father of hip-hop.

5

One day I was expecting my father to come home, but he never arrived. The next day, more of the same, nothing. For some reason, my mother was unfazed by my father's disappearance. This went on for days. In the meantime, everything was quite at home. My mother was relaxed. I wasn't being hit; it was really nice.

Then I started to feel depressed because a part of me was missing him, and I began to worry. I was happy because things at home were still good. I started to think and ask myself, *Maybe he was staying at some woman's place that he had taken me to. Did my mother chase him away?*

Bright early one morning, my mother woke me up and told me to get ready. Boy, did I hate going to school. My classmates would pick on me, and on top of that, my teachers would be mean to me. Oh, how I dread it.

My mother took me on the train then to a bus. I wondered where we were headed. I never questioned my mother. I knew better. She would get an evil look as though she was possessed. That look meant I was going to get them—that's right, the "Puerto Rican pela."

Finally we arrived at huge brick building with cars everywhere. We got on another bus which dropped us off to a long line of people. I thought this was where my mother would get the Welfare cheese. Oh, man! I was like in heaven. I was starting to get real excited. At the time in 1976, I don't know what it was, but the cheese back then tasted much different than it does know. So here we are, the line gets shorter and shorter. I was ecstatic. I couldn't wait. I looked up to my mother with a big smile on my face. She looked at me and smiled back. As we kept getting closer and closer, she said, "We're here to see your father."

I asked my mother, "Papi works at the cheese factory?"

She looked at me, and in a kind voice, she said these sweet words to me, "Pendejo, que cheese factory, quien told you eso!" Translation: "Stupid motherfucker, what cheese factory." My mother always spoke what we Spanish people call Spanglish. A language combination of Spanish and English.

Now I'm thinking, *Is this a trick? Is she trying to make me say something stupid, so when we get back home, I will be the recipient of the Puerto Rican pela?* So guess what I did? I answered her. I had to because as a child, we always do the opposite of what our parents tells us not to do. Go on. Tell a child, "Hey, don't touch that!" and see what happens.

Now I hear someone yelling "Step up." I've never seen such a horrific place in my life. Mind you, I was only a ripe six years old.

This tall man in a blue uniform yelled, "Everyone, welcome to Riker's Island."

"Adversity is the soil in which God breeds His champions"—Tommy Pickens (The Pastorpreneur)

6

I will never forget the feeling those officers made me feel walking in that place. I didn't know why or what was going on. I honestly thought it was for me. They were nasty to my mother and treated her like she had done something wrong. An officer patted me down, and then I walked through steel gates. I was scared thinking, *Why is my father here?* I remember seeing my father in the jumpsuit which barely fit him because of his big muscles (which is something I didn't inherit).

It was one of the happiest days. We hugged each other for a long time. My mother and father didn't speak much to each other while visiting him. We just hugged and kissed each other. I was only six, and when he finally spoke his first words to me, he said, "Papi, I want you to listen. I don't want you to come back and visit me in here, okay? This is the last place any man would want to be. Even the animals get better treatment in the doghouse."

Then he looked at my mother and said: "Alicia, do me the favor and don't bring my boy here to see me like this."

My mother responded with "Well, the next time you do your shit again, don't forget what you're leaving behind." I remember my father pouncing at her like a lion trying to grab her neck and the officers charged him with a nightstick, beating him and taking him away. I cried all the way home and started to resent my mother from that point on, not knowing why my father couldn't come home.

Let's fast forward. Just when I thought it couldn't get any worse, I woke up one morning and went to my mother's room. I was trying to wake her up; my mother was not waking up. I tried again and nothing. Mind you, I'm still only six years old. I can still remember it like it was yesterday. I went across the hallway to the project where my aunt lived. My cousin happened to answer the door. I told her, "Mamí's not waking up."

She ran into the apartment and saw my mom lying there peacefully on her bed. Now she's screaming her name and shaking her. No response. A second later, the landlord came into the apartment because of the screaming. He had my cousin bring some cooking oil. He poured it into her mouth. It looked like he was trying to drown her. At some point, the EMTs showed up and took her away. My aunt surprised me by taking me to the hospital to see my mother. It was the best feeling to know my mother didn't leave me. I'll tell you I don't know anything about God then, but I was grateful she was still with me. We really never talked about God or church at home. All I knew was I was Catholic. I felt like all this was my fault, so I kept telling myself and my mother that I would try to behave and be better. I didn't realize it wasn't my fault, but at that age, I believed it was.

JOSE MORALES

7

I had no choice but to grow up quickly. Circumstances dictated that I become very independent at such a young age. Especially living in the South Bronx where drugs and sex were on every corner of the block. On March 10, 1977, my brother Rich was born. I was so happy to have someone that I could love and protect. I made sure that he would not be treated the way I was. I slept with him, changed his diapers, and did as much as I could. I enjoyed it. I thought, *Who better than me to take care of him because I understood how to take care of him due to what I went through.* My parents continued the same drama. I would take my brother, lock us in my bedroom, and rock talk to him. I thought he would understand what's going on with my parents. The truth is, I too was a baby. We were both clueless. A year and a half later, my mother finally got tired of the abuse from my father. They were arguing, and I remember that for the first time, I got in between them, and I started to beg for my father to stop hitting my mother. I was crying. He started to cool off, but by this time, the cops had arrived and arrested him. This day was a turning point for all of us. As the cops took my father away, I remember him saying to my mother, "When

I get out of jail, I'm gonna come back, and I am gonna kill you." I was eight years old at this time.

Something about the way he said it, we knew he meant what he said. He was quite serious. That night my mother packed a suitcase. We took a train to stay with my grandfather who lived in Middletown, New York. It was a long night. At this age, with everything that was happening in my life and now my brother, I never really knew what was true happiness. I was already talking and acting in some way like my parents. I was a city kid with a filthy mouth, but I thought this was normal. My luck just kept changing for the worse. My mother told me she had to leave me with my grandpa. She took my brother with her back to the South Bronx. This was heartbreaking because I thought she abandoned me for good. I cried for days wondering what I did to chase her away. Three weeks later, she returned. I was very happy but worried again about the next time she would leave me behind again. Finally she found a place for us to live in. She enrolled me in Liberty School. Up to this point, there were no positive role models in my life. I was doomed—a total failure.

8

I'm now repeating third grade, again. I felt ashamed for having to repeat the grade, and then I was put in a bilingual class. I wasn't looking forward to it. There she was the woman that would change my life and make an impact: Mrs. Perez. I can't ever thank this woman enough. At this time, she was very pregnant. I loved coming to school just to see her. She was loving, caring compassionate, respectful, and very understanding. She started to notice my love for drawing. She was the first to guide me and started to enter me into art contests. I remember my first poster contest was for brushing your teeth. It was a monkey brushing his teeth upside down, and I won third place.

Another time, I won first place on a student stamp and received a twenty-five dollar prize. I was living the dream. Then one day I remember Mrs. Perez called me up to her desk. She started to talk to me, but as she was talking, I didn't realize she was covering her mouth with a piece of paper. I was trying to see over the paper to hear what she was saying, and then she stopped talking. She said to me it was okay to go back to my seat. At the time, I didn't think anything of it.

At the end of the day, she handed me an envelope to give to my mother.

A couple of days later, my mother and I ended up at some clinic in Goshen, New York, called CP Center. Thinking nothing of it, I was through some intense test. The next day, they called my mother, and she started to cry. She was still on the phone crying. She finally hung up and walked up to me and hugged me. She started to cry even harder. She was saying over and over how sorry she was for all the times she beat me. I didn't know what was going on. I kept telling her it was okay and I loved her. She broke down into more tears. She became a different woman and a better mother due to an act of kindness and compassion from my teacher. A teacher who went out of her way and noticed something was wrong with me. The clinic specialized in hearing. I learned that I was completely deaf in my right ear and moderately deaf in my left. When I was born, I had no hair above my right ear on what we thought was a huge birthmark. This was actually a burn that was caused by forceps that were used during delivery. In order to sterilize them, they were heated which resulted in the doctor burning my ear and somehow damaging my hearing. From the day I was told what happened to me, my mother finally grasped that my errant behavior wasn't my fault.

9

It became clear that all this time, I wasn't listening to my teachers before Mrs. Perez. It wasn't a language barrier. Instead, it was a handicap that prevented me from hearing. It all made sense when the only cartoon that I loved watching all those years that had helped me escape the craziness mentally were non-verbal. In return, this handicap that I've come to learn about was a blessing in disguise. It gave me my ability to love art which was a therapeutic way for me and the other. I was happy to know I wasn't doing anything wrong to get an everyday beating from my mother. The best of all, my mother became a better loving mother I always wanted to have.

I thought it was a blessing. I felt happy until I found out that I was being transferred into a special education classroom due to my hearing impair. It was then that I became classified in the State of New York as a handicapped person. Of course, I thought this was the end of the world. I was thinking the worst, and it was! I was fitted for a hearing aid that was as big as my entire ear, perhaps larger.

I felt totally insecure with my self-appearance. I already had long hair so that I could cover up the bald spot I had above my right ear. I remember neighborhood kids and family members making fun of me. It created anger issues. I started to hate kids that would say things that offended me. I would walk away crying. I was never a fighter. I hated my life and was just boiling with anger. I started my new class as an individual with special needs. I felt like I didn't belong. There's nothing wrong with me being selfish. I didn't want anything to do with special needs students. I always sat alone. It took a bully to set off something inside of me to stand up for a these students with special needs. He was making fun of a girl, Jane, from my class and how she walked. I got up, walked straight over to him, and told him to stop talking about her. He kept going. I told him a second time to stop. He said to me, "What is it to you? You're not handicapped. You don't walk funny."

I told him I am handicapped. He started to say something I don't remember what, but I grabbed him and started to punch him nonstop until the teachers came. Of course, I got detention and almost a butt whooping. I managed to explain to my mother, and she was cool with it. From time to time, I found myself defending those that were picked on—verbally, that is. It really irked and upset me when I realized how mean kids could be.

"Take your stumbling stone and turn them into your stepping-stones and PRESS4WARD"—Jose Morales (PRESS4WARD)

10

Four years later, we moved back to the South Bronx. This really hurt me mentally because I finally felt settled. I was happy and blessed to have those teachers during the time I lived in Middletown who were very caring. The year is 1982, and we were back in the South Bronx. Break dancing was hopping and graffiti was everywhere. This is where I started to blend in with anyone and everyone. I remember I was battled for fun and realize I was pretty good, so I began to dance for money. You see, even though my family partied every night and acted like every day was Friday, I fought very hard emotionally and mentally not be like them. I enjoyed the positive attention I was receiving from the people, and I started to tag up (graffiti) on public walls of the #5 train. I started to hang out with the wrong crow. Perhaps I was better off in Middletown.

I started to do bad stuff not realizing that I was really no different than some of my members of my own family. I would wander about, hang out until midnight on the streets, cut classes, and get chased by paddy wagons. I started dabbling with all kinds of new illegal activities and hanging out with older kids. Then I ran into Nelson.

Nelson was a lot older than I was. Nelson introduced me to hard drugs one night when I was fifteen. I remember hanging out in Crotona Park in the Bronx, drinking Private Stock beer at noon. By late evening, I was wasted. He took me home. I hit the bed hard just to sleep it off. A few hours later, I woke up still drunk. We went out drinking liquor and ended at some guy's apartment where he was having a party. There, I had my first experience with white line (cocaine). Oh, my God, what a horrible aftertaste. Still to this day, I hate to use nasal spray because it reminds me of the after-taste. Anyhow, I'm up all night sniffing, drinking, and smoking weed. Something inside me didn't want to do this. I wasn't really having fun, but I thought this would make me feel somewhat normal and not handicapped. No one knew about my imperfection. The next day, I remember feeling mentally, physically, and emotionally drained.

11

I remember that day well. I was taking a shower, and I heard someone come into the bathroom. It was my uncle, one of my mother's brother. I didn't pay any mind to him. I thought he just had to use the restroom. A few minutes went by and I peeked out because I wasn't sure if he was still there. He was still there and was in process of shooting heroin with his arm exposed and a rubber band in his left arm. His eyes were closed, and the syringe was in his arm. I panicked. I waited until he finished, so I could get out. This had me so damn scared. I went and told my stepfather. My stepfather told my mother which she then told her older brother Manny. This led to a confrontation between my uncle Manny beat the crap out of my uncle Carlos in the middle of the street. My uncle Manny was like the godfather in the drug world. I remember him telling me "a real drug dealer never uses his own product, only sells it. It's a sign of weakness." For him, this is how you start to lose control. Those that sell for you will come at you to try to take over; this is my life. I remember saying, "There's nothing wrong with the way I am," but at a very young age, I always felt there was something missing in my life. I just didn't know what it was yet.

At fifteen years old, I finally got skin graft surgery to remove the burn mark above my right ear at Lenox Hill Hospital in Manhattan. I was hoping that this will help me become more self-confident and not feel insecure about my appearance. I hope I would finally be able to have a normal haircut because up to that point, I always had long hair just to cover the bald spot above my ear. Though this did not help me with my hearing, it help me with my physical confidence. Little did I know and would not until later in life that it's not about appearances but about how I feel like a person inside. Throughout my teenage years into my twenties and thirties and now in my late forties, I have finally learned and accepted that I shouldn't feel ashamed of who I am. It is all about accepting who you are, finding out who you are, and taking that and pressing forward with what God gave you. I went through a lot and made many excuses for myself as to why I didn't amount to much as a result of my hearing problem. Stop listening to other people in your life telling you that you are worthless and you won't amount to much. After a while, you start to believe it. Once that happens, it is very difficult to bounce back because mentally, you start to believe it.

12

Separate yourself from anyone who does this to you or your children. If you are one of them, check yourself. Why do you have the need to belittle and degrade others? It is hard work to be nasty and bitter. Do not pass the torch of your problems and insecurities to the ones you claim to love and care for. That is a not the definition of caring. Th is a baggage that is spiritually draining; it is unnecessary weight. You will be in no shape or form to be productive for yourself, family, friends, job, coworker, or to anyone for that matter. I had to embrace my physical condition and learn what I can do is become a better person.

Let's start with individuals who really cannot defend for themselves. Individuals who are in far worse condition, physically and mentally. I want to help these people having lived the experience, the shame and humiliation. I realized that I want to make a difference in other people's lives regardless of whether it was a matter of hearing, seeing, walking, touching, speaking, or any disability that someone was living with. Life goes on and can be quite fulfilling. It is important that you make a difference. It does not cost you anything to say "Hi," "How are you," and "Have a good day." Small gestures like this can turn a day and even a life around. There are people with emotional and mental problems; that too is a handicap. Any condition that paralyzes you from believing in yourself and robs you from pressing forward and realizing your full potential requires positive intervention.

When I was in my late teens, I took a piece of advice from my mother: not to ever limit myself. You are no different from the next person, and whatever I do whether it is being a dishwasher, I should simply be the best dishwasher I can be. If I was custodian, to be the best custodian. Whatever I did, just be the best I could be at it and never be afraid of what people think because the worst thing I can do is nothing. Learn everything and anything, but most of all, respect everyone you cross paths with. It was something easy for me to do, however, in order to respect others, I had to start with respecting myself. I was finding it hard to even love myself with everything I had been through. At some point, I was having problems with making certain people feel special. It was a struggle for me. I worked in all types of jobs as a graphic designer, medical field, counselor, and many others. I was a hustler by nature. The one thing I can say is I never sold drugs even though that is what I was exposed to along with the lifestyle that accompanies it. There was something inside of me that made me still feel empty. By this point, I already went through a couple of breakups and divorce and had children by the age of eighteen. I was hot mess, but I knew that life must have more to offer. I did not know what it was.

13

In 2008, I was already a year in with the United States Department of Justice Federal Bureau of Prisons. I was working a unit that consisted of one hundred and fifty inmates in each block (housing unit). I was in the common area, and one of the duties was to observe and communicate with the inmates but not in a lengthy conversation manner. I notice one particular inmate in a wheelchair speaking about the Bible to another inmate. While observing the unit, I could overhear them saying how this book had changed their lives in the most positive way while being incarcerated. This really piqued my curiosity as to how a book really changes anyone's life. Mind you, I was not a religious guy. I never heard of the Bible growing up. The only time I heard of the Bible mentioned was during a funeral in a church. That day, I came across a coworker, and he started to share how he too was transformed by the Bible. I was so intrigued. I needed to know more. We eventually started to talk and share with each other what we had been through. I truly began to realize this was a missing piece all along since my childhood. I was at such peace; something inside of me was starting to understand my existence.

I began to understand the more I read and realized it was a purpose for my condition. There was a reason for my upbringing and all that I endured. Yes, it sounds awful but think about it, how would I know what good was without adversity and challenge? That goes for all of us. When we are in the midst of the storm, it is really hard to see the land. It is really molding and shaping us into the person we are or become. I can count the numerous times I thought I was not going to make it. I thought I would be better off quitting, giving up, and succumbing to my thoughts.

They don't really need me, and other dark and ugly thoughts along those lines went through my mind. Nobody even cares or notices me. I felt invisible. You are dead wrong! Trust me, when you think no one is watching, they are. When you think no one cares, they do. We just get consumed in our problems, our imperfections, and our worries—family, job, and the list goes on. We think no one is noticing us; they certainly are, and they too have the same concerns and issues. We are searching to look up to someone who can motivate and drive us to become someone better than we think possible. So for me at that time, believing in something I could not see was unfathomable. But there was something that kept tugging at my heart. What was it? What did I have to lose if this didn't work out? I would be in the same place as if nothing ever happened. I will tell you how I started. Find a way to love yourself. Talk about challenges; this was hard for me because I had so many complaints about myself. It was hard to see myself in a positive light. I had to think of ways to love myself. When I learned to love myself, I was able to inspire others to do the same.

"Do not let your past dictate who you are, but let it be a lesson to strengthen the person you aim to become"

14

These were questions and answer I put myself through in order to figure out who I am and quotes that lead me to question myself.

* Believe that I am special and unique.
* I am one in a million. There may be others that look like me, but there is only one me.
* What makes me special and unique?
* I must seek within myself and ask why I am special and unique.
* What unique qualities set me apart from everyone else?
* Let my faith overcome my fears.
* Learn how to make that special quality become your biggest asset.
* How can I use that quality to help better others?
* Be active; turn it into action. Be passionate about what I believe in.
* People will not understand you; continue to press forward.
* Be relentless with the passion that you have found within yourself. Run with it.

* Do not take advice from Mr. and Mrs. Know It All's, the ones who tell you what you need to do, but they do not apply it within their own lives. Do not listen to naysayers or haters because nothing is impossible.
* Eighty percent of people do not care about your problems, and 20 percent are happy you have them.
* Everyone wants to be right.
* Everyone wants to feel superior.
* Everyone likes to pass judgment (possibly without being aware of their hurtful action).

15

I am not here to motivate you. I am here to inspire you, to tell you the truth. There is a big difference here. Motivation gets you going, but the inspiration is what makes you move in a certain direction to act on, to press forward. I can go about all of the sad and depressing things that I went through in my life, but the truth is, I wouldn't change a thing. Adversity is what made the person I am today. Without it, I wouldn't know what I was capable of. It is how we grow and learn how to press forward into life. You're always going to encounter situations whether it is emotionally, physically, and mentally stressful and straining. Learn to use these encounters as a platform. Take your stumbling stones and turn them into your stepping stones. Whatever it is that's holding you back, it is imperative to believe in yourself. Work on being in love with the person you see in the mirror every day. The person who has been through so much but is still standing. Press forward on being your true self. Everyone else is already taken. These are the things I had to learn and realize about myself one day at a time. I continue to find myself one day at a time, step by step. I had to find myself and learn who I was. As I kept loving myself, this eventually started to show. The people around me that I loved and cared for deeply were also impacted, and they started to change their behavior. For some, it takes a lot of healing on their journey. For others, convincing themselves that they are worthy despite their physical, mental, or emotional state is liberating.

Now I have been working for the BOP for twelve years. In those twelve years, I have encountered and seen some crazy stuff. I wouldn't believe it unless I saw it with my own eyes. I definitely learned a lot working in an environment which is so inhumane. This place had shown me how to communicate effectively to be able to learn how to listen and not just hear, to see and not just look, and to understand the unbelievable. I have come across individuals who need to be in psychiatric institutional facilities and not a warehouse prison setting. These people needed some psychotropic medication. Some of them were here for petty crimes they had committed and received such a harsh sentences that morally did not fit the crime they committed. Some that are presumed innocent and some who really needed to be incarcerated were all warehoused together.

16

This environment has shaped and molded me in such a profound way. I have witnessed firsthand how a handful of staff but not all were so callous to other people's feelings, not just the inmates. I remember a lieutenant did something that really helped me relate to him. I was glad that I was not alone as to how I thought professionals should really conduct ourselves no matter what. Race, color, religion, or any other group—whether you are staff or an inmate—how you treat people is telling of who you really are. At the end of the day, we are all human and make mistakes. Some mistakes surely are worse than others, but mostly, the inmates I dealt with were minimum human beings and who showed remorse for their mistakes.

Some get caught but most do not. I remember in one particular instance that one inmate was going through some issues. I did not know the cause. I just happened to walk out from the cafeteria when I saw the lieutenant was standing still with his hands together in front of his duty belt listening to this upset inmate, speaking loudly, raising his voice. He was clearly angry. I walked over, and as I approached them, I witnessed the lieutenant speaking to the inmate in a respectful, calm voice requesting if he could ask him a question. The inmate said "Go ahead."

The lieutenant said, "In all of the time I have been standing here listening to you, have I raised my voice at you, or have I disrespected you?"

The inmate replied, "No."

The Lieutenant asked him, "So how do you expect anyone to listen to you when you are this worked up and expect to be heard or respected?" The inmate was quite for a second and looked down to the ground as he realized he was being irrational and ashamed of his behaviour. He proceeded to tell the lieutenant that it was not directed at him. He was angry and needed to vent. The inmate thanked the lieutenant, someone in his position for treating him like a human being and hearing him out in difficult moment. Still to this day, I never found out what the issue was, but what caught my attention was the lieutenant. By this time, he had been in the line of work for years and knew how to talk to the inmate, listen to their problems, and resolve issues all the while displaying respect and compassion for what inmates were going through. I view the lieutenant as a decent human being and professional and above all realized that the inmate was human no matter what the environment. It was not a sign of weakness on the lieutenant's behalf. Instead, I viewed it as a sign of integrity. The alternative that I have sadly witnessed all too frequently was someone with power, and in that position, simply escalating the matter and sending the inmate to solitary confinement.

17

At the end of the day no matter what crime an inmate has committed, they are still human and have emotions. The lieutenant used his discretion and, above all, his wisdom and compassion. I hope you did not miss the importance of the lieutenant's choice to use wisdom. A lot of us have too much knowledge but never apply any wisdom in our decision-making process. You have a choices. When it comes to making choices, whether you are unhappy and want better, the choice whether you are going to stop complaining about whatever is consuming your mind is yours. For many years, I always complained about my handicap until one day when I was on the school bus, a boy walked onto the bus, sat down across from me, and was so polite to everyone. This made me very happy. It put my life into perspective as this boy had no arms. He did everything utilizing his mouth and feet, and what stuck with me was that he was always happy and smiling.

I realize it wasn't my physical condition that kept me from being happy or doing the things I wanted to do. It was me, my mind-set. I was stopping myself from becoming anything positive in this world. He had a choice, and he chose not to let his handicap stop him. Rather, he embraced it and figured out how to be a positive force. There is so much we can become; the options are endless. We just refuse, at times, to believe that when we have negative influences in our lives telling us we will not amount to anything to believe otherwise. "You are a loser, and you will never change" are the words of losers. For the majority of us, we believe these naysayers. We believe the vitriol they spill when they speak to us. This can easily carry forward into all aspects of our lives, especially our family, occupation, and friendships.

Rule #1: Do not let people make you think or feel that you're number 2. We are all number 1 no matter your condition or circumstance. Trust me, I have been through several career paths and relationships mostly because I was unaware of my worth and place in the world. It took me overcoming many obstacles in the world to make me realize I was sick and tired of being sick and tired.

I got down on my knees. I was praying for God to just end my life and put me out of my misery. Something, however, was tugging at my heart to continue pressing forward. I started to do things I enjoyed doing. I started to go to the gym and focus on my health. I started to read in order to exercise my mind. I started to eat healthier to better my body. I started socializing with people who had positive attitudes that helped lift me mentally, emotionally, and spiritually. It is important that you free yourself of your insecurities and self-doubt. I had to learn this the hard way. This didn't happen overnight. It was a year-long journey. Yes, I am still learning and growing with each passing day. I wouldn't change anything about my past as it has laid the foundation for the current journey that I am on. I remember one day coming home, and my electricity had been shut off. I still pulled through, working things out with the electric company. I remember another occasion when my vehicle was repossessed. With a few phone calls, I found out it was a clerical error between the insurance companies. Other times, I don't have enough to get by, an empty fridge at home and wondering, *How am I going to feed my family?*

"I've experiences a lot of defeat, but I will not be defeated!!"—Jeremy Anderson (Motivational Speaker)

18

It felt like things were coming together one by one, and as the saying goes, "When it rains, it pours." I finally refused to sit and feel sorry for myself. It wasn't that I was not paying my bills or making enough money. In fact during this time, I came to find out I was the victim of a cyber breach that occurred due to my employer, Federal Government. Somehow they caused my personal information to be compromised. Talk about a nonstop roller coaster. I was absolutely ready to give up; when would the punches stop? All I could think about was my beautiful family. I realized that giving up was not option. I refused to let my fiancée and my children down or even worse, not be able to provide for them. I am truly blessed to have Stephanie, this wonderful woman, who is very supportive and loving. She has always stuck by my side through thick and thin. I just didn't want them to think that it is acceptable behavior to roll over and play dead. That is not what I want to instill in my children. I needed to set a strong example to teach my family that in life, you must press forward to get not only what you deserve but also what you want. It is yours. You just must press forward even when you feel the cards are stacked against you. I have learned that I can't blame anyone for my failures. A true leader takes responsibility for his failures and mishaps, learn from them, and keeps it moving. As the patriarch of my family, I was that leader. I implore you to stop wasting time pondering the past. You only live once, and today marks the first day of the rest of your life. Make it count.

Decisions sometimes hurts. That does *not* mean it was necessarily the wrong decision. Sometimes decisions are hurtful to ourselves, but in the long run, they are the right ones to make for ourselves and our family. The only way I was able to learn was that it was the right decision for me. But sometimes others did not understand and felt like it was wrong of me. The life you are living now is about you and what is best for your immediate family. It is *not* about those who pass judgment. I was too consumed worrying about what people were thinking rather than focusing on me. I learned to stay away from negative energy, no matter who it was giving of the negativity. Stay away from negative people because they have all the negative outcomes to your solutions. They will only tell you that you can't because they know that *they* can't. Still, I treated these people with kindness and respect because I always try to treat others the way I would like to be treated in return. Trust me, it is a blessing I've learned, especially when you do it from your heart. Meaning it and doing so because it is who you are expecting nothing in return. That is the key.

19

I remember being consistent with treating people with respect in this particular gathering I attended. An older gentleman who was always watching, but I never noticed him watching me, one day started to talk to me. And we started to share stories about our jobs, family, and politics. We began building a friendship. One day he shared that he owns a company and was looking to invest in a project. As a result of our conversation, he told me that instead, he was considering helping me get my message out and advancing my movement of kindness and perseverance. I thought this guy was insane, so I just yessed him to death. I just thought he was being nice. After a few more conversation, he gave me his business contact number and told me to call him. Of course, I procrastinated and delayed it for a few days. I spoke to another guy I knew that knew about this person, and I was told he was the real deal. Of course, I followed up that stamp approval. The next day I called the man, and I am glad I did because shortly after the call, I ended up with a check from him which allowed me to open my business. I started to press forward through this act of kindness and his belief in me. It was a beautiful gesture and overwhelming at the same time. A blessing all at once. It created opportunities and opened doors that I thought would be impossible to open. He saw I was passionate about my message when no one else did. He saw something, heard, and believed in me and my message. I was thrown off to think that some of my friends and family had no faith in what I felt was important to spread among others. A complete stranger whom I had known for an extremely short period of time believed in me enough to bless me. I could have never imagined this. Along with two other wonderful people in my life, Mike and YG, who were there believing in this project an investing in me. This is how my journey to spread my story and core values became what it is today. Now it is your turn to create change. Change among yourself, family, and friends. *Press4ward* and bless others with this message.

Your failures are someone else's blessings. Teach and press forward about how you too overcame your setbacks, your mistakes, and remember it's never too late to start from where you currently are no matter how bleak you view your situation may be. There is no problem with falling but don't settle there. When you are motivated, you influence others. Be it at work with family or friends or simply strangers. Be a leader and not a boss. A leader inspires respect, but a boss instils fear. There are too many bosses in the world and all they do is manage their employees horribly while also instilling fear. What this world needs are leaders to inspire and innovate you—to encourage you to think outside of the box. A leader will recognize your natural gifts. Press forward and become an advocate for those who think less of themselves.

It is never too late. A mentor of mine once said, "We spend so much time worrying about what others people think, but they don't even care about you." At the end of your life on earth, do you think they're going to think or care about you? You must live for you, your family, close friends, and the legacy to make a difference.

20

I have to tell you, he is right on point. The reason I say that is because I remember watching on television the funeral service of John McCain, and something changed my way of thinking it took me to another level. In fact, it was President Obama when he started to read a quote from Hemmingway, "Today is only one day in all the days that will ever be, but what will happen in all the other days that ever come can depend on what you do today." Do not let your past dictate who you are, but let it be a lesson to strengthen the person you aim to become.

Change your thinking, and behavior will change with it. It is very important to know that every positive behavior starts in your mind. You mentally need to adjust your thinking. I had to learn this the hard way. I, for one, was a very stubborn young man, so it took me a while to get it, and it wasn't easy. I had to figure out what really worked for me. I was living a down spiral life. At any given time, I could have encountered some adversity one way or the other. I began to think, *What was it that I was doing wrong? Why wasn't I getting it?*

I thought of these every time I was in the same place over and over. I then thought maybe I should write it all down—

the good qualities I have—but this was a challenge back then because at the time, I wasn't confident with myself. I struggled to see the potential within me. But eventually as I started to write them down, I was pretty surprised of the things I wrote. I began to look better to myself. I then wrote what I don't like about myself. And, of course, I had more on the negative side than I did in the positive side. This is where I was able to see that writing it down was helpful. Everything I was complaining about had to do all with my mind. I started to see how I have a choice, a choice that can benefit me and change my whole attitude of how I view myself, my surrounding, and what I allowed in my life. I realized that I am that person who needs to see it and that hearing it was not working for me.

There are people who are different, but as for me, I found out it was seeing. It was key. Though I may have heard it a thousand times, it went in one ear out the other. It's funny how we need to get mentally beaten up before we figure out that you're really mentally fighting with yourself all along. I discovered that the mind is a wonderful organ that we fail to tap into. I started to find out more and more about what was hurting me, and when I started getting mentally get in gear, I was able to see that my attitude toward certain things in life was making more sense. I stopped being scared of what others thought about me or even said. This was the point of no return, even if the decision I made was wrong. I had to learn what I got out of it and what would I do differently. Little by little, my confidence had become more and more positive. My past mistakes started to become the best lessons in my life. I understood that in order to become effective in my personal life and with my surroundings, I needed to understand that whatever adversity would strike at any giving time, I had to figure out how I was going to take control and not allow it to control me. I understood that there is only one way to succeed—and that is to *press4ward* at all costs.

21

It's early January 2019, and President Trump and Congress are at an impasse over a *wall*. The government is shut down, at least partially. The adversity continues. The government shutdown hits home. There's nothing worse than coming to work and not knowing when you're getting paid. Here I was thinking, *When is this whole thing going to get resolved?* I had to come up with different alternative to make ends meet, a way that will allow me to make money legally without getting into any nonsense with my job. I need to provide for my family. So I registered online to receive a certificate to become a daycare teacher's assistant and ended working with my fiancée, Stephanie, at her job. Thank God she was able to speak with her boss in terms of offering me the job. At the time, her boss was going through a rough period trying to get a reliable staff that would last at her daycare facility. She knew who I was, and it made for a good opportunity. A second income to compensate for the income I was not receiving from the government was much needed at such a time. At one point, we were living off two incomes. And here we are now, living off one. It was pretty tough.

Our bills started to pile up weekly, and all the government was doing was giving out online resources that were not guaranteed. It's a punch in the gut. I remember thinking, *I need to come up with something like now.* Here we are two car payments behind. The electric company is about to shut off our electricity and back up on child support obligation. We need to pay rent, cable, and needed gas to go to and from work because I still have to show up knowing I wasn't getting paid by the government. A lot of things just kept adding on, and we had to kind of spread the little extra income that we were getting just to feed the family. While all this is unfolding, I kept pressing forward with this book, believing that it's my mission. I wanted to utilize this experience I was going through to be able to live and tell others to keep the faith. It's never the end unless and until you give up, and even then, you should remember why you started to pursue the vision and dream that was pressing in your heart. I hear one of my mentors say, "Give a man the answer, and he'll have only a temporary solution. Teach the principles that led you to that answer, and he will be able to create his own solutions in the future" (Eric Thomas, the hip-hop preacher). I so truly believe this. This was one of the main reasons I feel compelled to pursue a new career as a motivational speaker—to be able to give more than just talks. I want to innovate, inspire, and motivate people who need to understand that all obstacles that seem a hindrance can be converted to something positive. Adversity is what makes you who you are and what you are capable of. These are lessons that will strengthen you.

What I am getting is this: Continue to learn, read, and study everything that you can get your hands on. It's up to you if you want it or not. Don't blame others for your laziness; the world owes you nothing! It may be a rude awakening, but this world doesn't owe you. If you want it, get up, *press-4ward*, and go get it. I remember my mother saying, "Learn everything and anything because you'll never know when adversity will strike." If you're well-equipped and can hold your ground, you will make it. Don't go comparing yourself to someone else as to why he or she has it and you don't. Remember, they are not you. This is what makes you one of a kind.

"Character is revealed during adversity, not in good times"—Setema Gali (Entrepreneur/Superball Champion)

22

It very imperative that you don't contradict what you believe and who you are. Make sure your talk lines up with your walk. I was guilty of this at one point. I would talk the talk, but when it was time to walk the walk, it never lined up. This very bad, especially when you're expecting people that you love and care about—whether it's a loved one, coworker, friends, or family to look up to you. I'll give you an example: If you tell to your spouse you're going to do the dishes when you get home, then do them. Don't procrastinate by making excuses and then never get to it until later, or even worse, don't even do them at all because you're way tired. Something this small and simple may not look like a big deal to you, but it will for spouse. It's not like your significant other can't do it. I am pretty sure they can. It's the principle behind it; if you give your word, then stand by what you say. At one time, I didn't realize the significance and the big deal, but what I have come to learn and realize is that I was creating doubts to my woman. She pointed out and corrected me how every time I mentioned I was going to do something, I either started and never finish, or don't do it at all. I got so bent out of place, but you know what, it was the truth.

Sometimes you need that person to hold you accountable for your action. This made me really check myself; my intentions were good. I started off with intentions to complete my task I was driven. But somehow, I didn't finish. This is not a good thing. Then you go through life all the time saying what you're going to do, but you really don't come through for some lame reason. So I started to push myself with small task from start to finish, and I progressively started to take on bigger task, and the next thing I knew, I was actually feeling positive and good that I was able to execute anything and everything I said I was going to do. That started to build a positive vibe and outlook around my family, friends, and coworkers. I started showing that I am a man of my word. So whatever you put off in your life, whether it's a project or something for someone or even a passion that you always wanted to do, do it! Get in there and finish what you started! I guaranteed that you're going to feel good about yourself and wonder why in the world you had not done it sooner. *Press4ward!*

23

It took me quite some time to learn how to be mentally strong. I needed to understand that in order to press forward in anything I wanted to accomplished in life, I first needed to mentally convince myself that I am worthy and deserve to be at peace with myself. I looked up the word *peace*. The definition of it means "Freedom from turmoil and war." This is precisely what we go through when we are not mentally understanding how much we need to believe in ourselves as well as to love ourselves. We go through the turmoil and war by listening to people who make you feel guilty in some type of way and making you believe that you're not capable of accomplishing anything in life all because they can't. The truth is, they can too. If they only understood how powerful the mind is and how to become mentally free, they would spend less time holding others back and would become more encouraging to others. Don't fall victim to this. Learn that you are in control of your mind and that you have a choice.

A trapped mind is horrible feeling; it paralyzes you from being emotionally, spiritually, mentally, and guilt free. This makes you unproductive. It is very important that you understand that you can free yourself and be at peace. Find ways that you can become effective and productive. If this means staying away from people who are not encouraging, then so be it. It sounds harsh, but it's the reality. Don't waste your time with anyone who is always complaining and saying, "I can't do this" or "I can't do that," "Why me, God?" blah, blah, blah, blah.

I was that guy and believe me when I tell you that this is the most negative and ugliest thing you can do to yourself. Be willing to take the first step. Know that you have what it takes to be at peace with yourself. For sure some people are not always going to see eye to eye with your inner peace; and, of course, they're going say lies about you or gossip about you and even do things toward you to break you. This will prove that you're on the right path and that there's something about how you're conducting and thinking that is affecting those who don't understand what it's like to be mentally free. Stop feeling sorry for yourself! Stop worrying about what they are going to think about you. An unhealthy mind is an unhealthy life. If you're not mentally fit, the rest of your body is not going to be either granted they are people who really can't find mental peace no matter what they do. There's help for them as well. The important thing is that you find a way to speak to someone who can help you. This too is a disability, and it must be addressed so that you can find a way to become mentally healthy and proactive in your daily living. I've seen and known so many individuals who blow it off to the point where it was uncontrollable, and the end result was them taking their own life. If you feel like you need more than just talking to friend or a family member, please seek professional help. This doesn't make you any less of a person or weak; it makes you smart and ahead of the game. Doing something is better than doing nothing. The fact that you're reading this book should tell you your worth and what you are capable of overcoming. Continue to PRESS4WARD 2NXTLEVEL and finish strong.